KU-350-572

Family Circle

Classic Essential

SEAFOOD

The Family Circle Promise of Success

Welcome to the world of Confident Cooking, created for you in the
Family Circle Test Kitchen, where recipes are double-tested by our team of home
economists to achieve a high standard of success.

M U R D O C H   B O O K S®
Sydney • London • Vancouver • New York

Seafood Sauces

These sauces are based on the French classic, mayonnaise. You can make your own, or buy one of the many ready-made brands.

Classic Mayonnaise

Place 2 egg yolks, 1 teaspoon smooth mustard, salt and ground black pepper in a small bowl. Using electric beaters or a balloon whisk, beat until thick. Slowly add 1 tablespoon white wine vinegar or lemon juice, beat until combined well. Add 1¼ cups good quality oil, drop by drop, to egg mixture, whisking or beating constantly. After about half the oil has been used, add the remainder in a thin stream, whisking or beating constantly. When mixture is thick and creamy, add an extra tablespoon of vinegar or lemon juice. Taste for seasonings; adjust with lemon, vinegar, salt, pepper or mustard.

To make in a food processor ~ Place yolks and vinegar in food processor. With motor running, add oil slowly in a thin stream. Process until thick and creamy. Add seasonings to taste.

Vary the flavour with different oils (good quality): try light olive oil, or peanut, sunflower or safflower oil. Store mayonnaise in airtight conatiner in refrigerator for up to 2 weeks. Makes 1½ cups.

Andalouse

Cook ¼ red capsicum and ¼ green capsicum, skin side-up, under preheated grill until skin blackens and blisters. Remove, cool then peel away skin. Chop the flesh finely, add it to 1½ cups of mayonnaise and stir. Add 1–2 tablespoons tomato puree. Garnish with chopped red capsicum.

Remoulade

Combine 1 1/2 cups mayonnaise, 2 finely chopped gherkins, 1 teaspoon each chopped capers and chopped chives, 1 tablespoon each chopped fresh tarragon and chopped fresh parsley, 1 teaspoon French mustard, and 1–2 teaspoons anchovy essence or finely chopped anchovies. Garnish with anchovies.

Tartare Sauce

Combine 1 1/2 cups mayonnaise, 1 finely chopped gherkin, 1 teaspoon chopped capers, 1 tablespoon each chopped fresh chives, chopped fresh tarragon or chervil, and chopped fresh parsley, 1/4 teaspoon smooth mustard and 1 tablespoon grated onion. Top with capers.

Thousand Island

Combine 1 1/2 cups mayonnaise, 1 tablespoon sweet chilli sauce, 1–2 tablespoons tomato sauce, 1/4 red capsicum and 1/4 green capsicum, finely chopped, 1 tablespoon chopped fresh chives and 1/2 teaspoon sweet paprika. Sprinkle with paprika.

Green Goddess

Combine 1 1/2 cups mayonnaise, 4 mashed anchovy fillets, 4 finely chopped spring onions, 1 crushed garlic clove, 1/4 cup chopped fresh parsley, 1/4 cup finely chopped chives, and 1 teaspoon sweet chilli sauce. Top with parsley.

Top row, from left: Tartare Sauce, Remoulade, Cocktail Sauce. Bottom row, from left: Andalouse, Green Goddess and Thousand Island sauces

Cocktail Sauce

Combine 1/4 cup tomato sauce with 1 cup mayonnaise, 1 drop tabasco, 2 teaspoons worcestershire sauce, 1/2 teaspoon lemon juice, salt and black pepper. Garnish with lemon .

～ Poached Atlantic Salmon with Hollandaise Sauce ～

Preparation time:
20 minutes
Total cooking time:
10 minutes

Serves 4

1 cup white wine	***Hollandaise Sauce***
2 cups fish stock	3 egg yolks
1 tablespoon lemon	125 g butter, melted
juice	and hot
1 large slice onion	1/2 teaspoon grated
4 Atlantic salmon	lemon rind
cutlets, 2.5 cm thick	1 tablespoon lemon
fresh dill, to garnish	juice

1 ～ Place wine, stock, lemon juice and onion slice in shallow pan. Bring to boil; reduce heat to simmer.

2 ～ Place salmon cutlets in single layer in simmering stock. Poach fish gently for about 7 minutes or until fish is just cooked.

3 ～ Remove from pan; drain on paper towels. Cover fish with foil to keep warm.

4 ～ **To make Hollandaise Sauce:** Place egg yolks in food processor; process for 10 seconds. With motor running pour hot and bubbling butter in slow stream onto egg. Discard white butter residue. Add grated lemon rind and juice; process for another 30 seconds or until sauce thickens. Serve immediately. Makes 2/3 cup.

5 ～ Arrange fish on serving dish. Serve with hollandaise sauce and garnish with fresh dill.

Note ～ Sauce is best made just before serving. However, it may be prepared up to 2 days in advance. Store in airtight container in refrigerator. Reheat by standing in dish placed over pan of gently simmering water. Cook salmon cutlets just before serving.

Variation ～ Ocean trout cutlets may be used in place of salmon. Or you may prefer to use a large salmon fillet or whole salmon, including the head. If using a whole salmon it is best to skin the fish after poaching. If serving whole salmon cold, leave in the stock until cooled; skin when cool.

Remove salmon cutlets from pan and drain on paper towels.

With motor running pour hot butter slowly into the food processor.

Poached Atlantic Salmon with Hollandaise Sauce

～ Fritto Misto di Mare ～

Preparation time:
30 minutes
Total cooking time.
12 minutes

Serves 4

Batter
1 cup self-raising flour
¼ cup cornflour
salt and pepper
1 tablespoon oil
1 cup water

500 g fish fillets, boned,
cut into 5 cm strips
12 sardines, heads and
bones removed
(see Note)

8 raw medium king
(large) prawns,
shelled
8 scallops, cleaned and
deveined
1 calamari hood, cut
into rings
flour for coating
oil for deep frying
tartare sauce (see
page 3), to serve
lemon wedges, to serve

1～To make Batter:
Sieve the flours, salt and pepper into a bowl; make a well in the centre. Combine oil and water; gradually whisk into flour until a smooth batter is formed.
2～Dry the prepared seafood on paper towels. Dip seafood in flour; shake off excess.
3～ Heat the oil in large deep pan until moderately hot. Coat a few pieces of seafood at a time with batter; gently lower into hot oil with tongs or a slotted spoon. Cook for 2–3 minutes or until golden brown and crisp.

Remove; drain on paper towels. Keep warm and cook remaining seafood. Serve accompanied with a bowl of tartare sauce and lemon wedges.
Note～ The seafood for this dish may be prepared several hours ahead; cover and keep in the refrigerator. To prepare fresh sardines, remove the heads and split them open down the belly; clean with salted water. Ease the backbone out with your

fingers and cut the backbone at the tail end with sharp scissors. Pat sardines dry.

Prepare sardines by easing out backbone with fingers; cut off at tail end of bone.

Gradually whisk combined oil and water into flour to form a smooth batter.

Fritto Misto di Mare

Dip the seafood in the flour and shake off any excess.

Drain cooked, golden brown seafood on paper towels; keep warm.

～ Tuna Mornay ～

Preparation time:
15 minutes + standing
Total cooking time:
35 minutes

Serves 4

1¹/₂ cups milk	¹/₄ teaspoon nutmeg
1 bay leaf	¹/₃ cup cream
1 onion slice	¹/₄ cup finely chopped
5 whole black	fresh parsley
peppercorns	¹/₂ cup grated cheddar
60 g butter	cheese
1 onion, finely chopped	salt and freshly ground
1 stick celery, finely	black pepper, to taste
chopped	¹/₂ cup fresh
¹/₄ cup plain flour	breadcrumbs
425 g can tuna,	¹/₂ cup grated cheddar
drained, flaked, juice	cheese, extra
reserved	paprika, to taste

1.～Preheat oven to moderate 180°C. In a small pan heat milk, bay leaf, onion slice and peppercorns. Bring to boil; remove from heat, cover, and let stand to infuse for 15 minutes. Strain and reserve milk.

2.～Heat butter in medium pan, add finely chopped onion and celery. Cook, stirring, for 5 minutes, or until onion is soft. Add flour and stir for 1 minute until mixture is bubbly. Add combined reserved milk and tuna juice gradually; stir constantly over low heat until mixture boils and thickens. Simmer over low heat for 5 minutes.

3.～Add nutmeg, cream, finely chopped parsley and grated cheese. Stir 2 minutes until cheese is melted. Remove from heat; add flaked tuna and salt and pepper; stir to combine.

4.～Spoon mixture into a 3-cup greased ovenproof dish. Sprinkle top with the combined breadcrumbs, extra grated cheese and paprika. Bake for 15 minutes. Remove from oven and place dish under preheated grill for 2 minutes to brown the breadcrumb mixture.

Note～Mornay may be made several hours ahead, refrigerated, and reheated. It may be used as a filling for pancakes or pastry cases.

Variation～You may use canned salmon, if preferred.

Add combined warm milk and tuna juice to pan after flour has cooked for 1 minute.

Remove pan from the heat and add the drained and flaked tuna.

Tuna Mornay

~ Lobster Bisque ~

Preparation time:
20 minutes
Total cooking time:
1 hour 20 minutes

Serves 4–6

1 raw lobster tail, about 400 g	1 tablespoon tomato paste
90 g butter	2 tomatoes, peeled, seeded and chopped
1 large onion, chopped	1 litre fish stock
1 large carrot, chopped	2 tablespoons rice flour or cornflour
1 stick celery, chopped	1/2 cup cream
1/4 cup brandy	salt and freshly ground black pepper
1 cup white wine	fresh oregano leaves and paprika, to serve
6 sprigs fresh parsley	
1 sprig fresh thyme	
2 bay leaves	

1 ~ Remove meat from lobster tail, wash and retain shell. Chop the lobster meat, cover and refrigerate.

2 ~ Heat butter in a large pan. Add onion, carrot and celery. Cook over low heat for 20 minutes, stirring occasionally, until vegetables are softened but not brown.

3 ~ In a small pan heat brandy; set alight and carefully and quickly pour over vegetables. Shake the pan until flame dies down. Add white wine and lobster shell. Increase heat, boil mixture until it has been reduced by half.

4 ~ Add parsley, thyme, bay leaves, tomato paste, tomato, and fish stock. Simmer without lid for 45 minutes, stirring occasionally.

5 ~ Strain mixture through a fine sieve or muslin, pressing gently down to extract all the liquid. Discard vegetables and shells.

6 ~ Return liquid to cleaned pan. Blend rice flour or cornflour with the cream. Add to the liquid. Stir over medium heat until thickened. Add lobster meat, season to taste. Cook gently without boiling about 10 minutes or until lobster meat is just cooked. Garnish with oregano leaves and paprika and serve.

Note ~ Can be made up to a day ahead and refrigerated. Reheat gently. Do not freeze. The long cooking time ensures optimum flavour for this delicate soup.

Use scissors to cut lobster shell so that meat can be removed easily.

Add white wine and lobster shell to brandy and vegetables in pan.

Lobster Bisque

Strain the mixture in a sieve, making sure to press down to extract juices.

Add combined flour and cream to reserved juice in pan.

～Trout with Almonds ～

Preparation time:
25 minutes
Total cooking time:
10 minutes

Serves 2

2 rainbow trout	2 tablespoons lemon juice
flour for coating	1 tablespoon finely
60 g butter	chopped fresh parsley
1/4 cup flaked	salt and freshly ground
almonds	pepper, to taste

1 ～Wash trout, pat dry with paper towels. Open trout out skin side up. Using a rolling pin, run along backbone starting from tail, pressing gently down. Turn trout over; using scissors, cut through backbone at each end of fish. Lever the backbone out. Check for any remaining bones. Trim fins with scissors.
2 ～Coat fish with flour. In a large frying pan heat 30 g of the butter; add fish. Cook 4 minutes each side or until golden brown. Remove fish and place on heated serving plates. Cover with foil.
3 ～Heat remaining butter; add flaked almonds and stir until almonds are a light golden brown. Add lemon juice, parsley, salt and pepper; stir until sauce is heated through. Pour over trout and serve immediately.
Note ～ Trout may be boned several hours ahead and refrigerated.

～ Stuffed Sardines ～

Preparation time:
20 minutes
Total cooking time:
30 minutes

Serves 4–6

1 kg fresh sardines	1/2 teaspoon sugar
1/4 cup olive oil	1 tablespoon finely
1/2 cup soft white	chopped fresh parsley
breadcrumbs	2 spring onions, finely
1/4 cup sultanas	chopped
1/4 cup pine nuts	salt and freshly ground
20 g can anchovies,	black pepper
drained and mashed	lemon wedges, to serve

1 ～Preheat oven to moderate 180°C. Cut the heads from fish. Split open belly of each sardine and remove insides. Lever off each backbone with fingers by gently pulling away from flesh. Cut off at tail end of bone. Wash in salted water and dry on paper towels.
2 ～Heat half the oil in a frying pan. Add breadcrumbs; cook quickly until lightly brown. Drain crumbs on paper towels.
3 ～Place half the crumbs in a bowl, stir in sultanas, pine nuts, mashed anchovies, sugar, parsley, spring onions, salt and pepper. Stuff about 2 teaspoons of mixture into each sardine cavity.
4 ～Place stuffed

Trout with Almonds (top) and Stuffed Sardines

sardines side by side into a well greased baking dish in a single layer. Sprinkle any remaining stuffing over the top of sardines with the reserved cooked breadcrumbs. Drizzle the reserved olive oil over top. Bake for 30 minutes. Serve sardines accompanied by lemon wedges.

Note ∼ Sardines may be prepared several hours ahead and refrigerated. Cook just before serving.

∼ Salmon Croquettes ∼

Preparation time:
**40 minutes +
refrigeration time**
Total cooking time:
10 minutes

Makes 15

90 g butter
3/4 cup plain flour
1 1/2 cups milk
2 x 210 g cans red
    salmon, drained, juice
    reserved
1/4 cup finely chopped
    fresh parsley
2 spring onions, finely
    chopped

2 teaspoons lemon juice
salt and freshly ground
    black pepper
plain flour for dusting
2 eggs, lightly beaten
dry breadcrumbs
oil for deep frying
lime wedges, to serve
mango chutney, to
    serve

1 ∼ Melt butter in medium pan; add flour. Stir over medium heat 1 minute; blend in combined milk and reserved salmon juice. Stir over medium heat until mixture boils and thickens. Reduce heat; simmer 3 minutes. Mixture will be thick.
2 ∼ Remove skin and bones from salmon and flake with a fork. Add salmon, parsley, spring onions, lemon juice, salt and pepper to flour mixture; stir to combine. Spread mixture onto a shallow tray, cover and refrigerate until firm.

3 ∼ Place flour onto a flat dish, eggs in a shallow dish and breadcrumbs onto a flat dish. Drop heaped tablespoons of mixture onto flour, mould into croquette shapes. Dip in egg; coat with the breadcrumbs. Refrigerate again for at least 1 hour.
4 ∼ Heat oil in a deep heavy based pan to moderately hot. Lower a few croquettes into hot oil using tongs or a slotted spoon. Cook 3–4 minutes or until golden brown. Drain on paper

towels; keep warm while cooking remainder. Serve with lime wedges and mango chutney.
Note ∼ Croquettes may be prepared several hours ahead. Uncooked croquettes can be frozen for up to one month.

Using fingers, carefully remove skin and bones from salmon.

Mould the salmon mixture into croquette shapes after coating with flour.

Salmon Croquettes

～ Crab Mayonnaise ～

Preparation time:
15 minutes
Total cooking time:
Nil

Serves: 4

3 x 170 g cans white crab meat	2 teaspoons white wine vinegar
1/2 cup whole egg mayonnaise	3 spring onions, finely chopped
1 tablespoon tomato sauce	2 tablespoons finely chopped fresh parsley
1/2 teaspoon worcestershire sauce	1/4 cup thick cream, whipped
dash tabasco sauce	salt and freshly ground black pepper
1 tablespoon olive oil	2 ripe avocados

1 ～ Drain crab meat and squeeze out excess juice; discard juice and place meat in a bowl. Cover and refrigerate.

2 ～ In a small bowl, whisk together the mayonnaise, tomato sauce, worcestershire sauce, tabasco, olive oil, vinegar, spring onions and parsley. Fold in whipped cream. Season with salt and black pepper, to taste. Cover and chill well.

3 ～ Just before serving, fold the mayonnaise mixture through the crabmeat. Halve the avocados; remove stone. Carefully remove half the avocado pulp from each avocado half; chop pulp roughly and fold through the crabmeat mixture. Serve the mayonnaise and avocado mixture piled on top of the avocado halves. Garnish with extra black pepper, if desired.

Note ～ Mayonnaise can be made several hours ahead (see page 2), if desired. The crabmeat mixture can also be prepared several hours before use and stored, covered, in the refrigerator. Crab Mayonnaise is not suitable for freezing. Fresh crab meat may be used in this recipe, if you prefer.

Drain crab meat and squeeze out any excess juice.

Fold the whipped cream into the mayonnaise mixture.

Crab Mayonnaise

Halve the avocados and carefully remove the stone.

Fold the chopped avocado through the crabmeat mixture.

～ Sushi & Sashimi ～

Sushi consists of vinegared rice and, most often, seafood. If it's made as a roll, it is usually wrapped in nori (seaweed). Sashimi is raw, very fresh seafood served with a dipping sauce. Unusual ingredients, such as kombu, may be found in Japanese food stores.

Sushi

To make vinegared rice ～ Rinse 2 cups short-grain rice in a fine strainer or colander. under running water, until the water runs clear. Place rice and 2 cups of water in a medium pan and set aside to soak for about 10 minutes. Place lid on pan, bring rice to boil, reduce heat to low and simmer gently for 8–10 minutes. Remove from heat and leave to stand for 15 minutes with lid on. Spread rice on a shallow dish or tray and cool to room temperature. Combine 2 tablespoons each of rice vinegar and caster sugar, and $1/2$ teaspoon of salt in a small pan. Heat gently to dissolve sugar. Sprinkle over the rice. Use at once.

To assemble Sushi ～ Combine 2 teaspoons rice vinegar and $1/4$ cup water. Use this mixture to keep hands moist when working with rice. Toast 5 sheets of nori seaweed by passing each sheet over a low gas flame or hotplate two or three times. Place the toasted seaweed, shiny side down, on a bamboo mat. Place one-fifth of the rice over a toasted nori sheet, leaving a 2 cm edge. Spread a very small layer of wasabi paste (very hot horseradish paste) in a thin line down centre of rice. Cut 125 g sashimi tuna or smoked salmon into thin strips. Place one-fifth on top of the wasabi. Top with some Japanese pickled ginger or vegetables and finely chopped cucumber or spring onion. Using the bamboo mat as a guide, carefully roll sushi enclosing in the rice the ingredients placed in the centre. Press nori to seal edges. Using a sharp bladed or electric knife, cut roll into 2.5 cm rounds. Repeat the process with remaining ingredients.

Nigiri Sushi

Clean, skin, bone and slice 500 g very fresh raw seafood, such as tuna, salmon, squid or cooked prawns, into 5 mm thick slices. Place a small amount of wasabi on the centre of each fish slice. Combine 1 teaspoon rice vinegar and 1/4 cup water and use it to moisten your hands to make handling the rice easier. Form a ball of vinegared rice (see under Sushi for recipe). Press a fish slice and ball of rice together to form a neat rectangle, with fish wrapped just around rice. Repeat process with remaining seafood. Arrange on a shallow platter and serve with soy sauce for dipping.

Sashimi

Place a selection of very fresh seafood, such as tuna, salmon, kingfish, ocean trout, snapper, whiting, bream or jewfish (sea bass), in the freezer. Chill until fish is sufficiently firm to be cut thinly and evenly into slices about 5 mm in width. Use a very sharp knife and cut with an even motion, taking care not to saw. Place sashimi on a flat platter and serve with a dipping sauce and garnish.

Dipping Sauces

1. Combine 1/4 cup each of lemon juice and soy sauce in a small bowl.
2. Combine 1/2 cup each lemon juice and soy sauce, 6 teaspoons each of mirin and sake, one 5 cm piece kombu (dried kelp) and 1 table-spoon dried bonito flakes. Refrigerate sauce for 24 hours and strain before serving.

Tuna Sashimi with Miso Sauce

In a small bowl whisk ogether 2 tablespoons of miso paste, 1 egg yolk, 1 teaspoon sake, 1 teaspoon English mustard powder, 1 teaspoon rice wine vinegar, 2 teaspoons mirin, and about 4–5 tablespoons of water. Place the bowl over a pan of gently simmering water and whisk until the mixture thickens. Place in the refrigerator until required. Serve with fresh tuna.

Top row: Sushi. Bottom row, from left: Nigiri Sushi (using salmon and prawns), Dipping Sauce, Sashimi and Miso Sauce.

～ Seafood Tempura ～

Preparation time:
40 minutes
Total cooking time:
15 minutes

Serves 4

Batter
2 egg yolks
200 ml iced water
1 cup plain flour

Dipping Sauce
1 cup dashi
1/3 cup mirin or dry
 sherry
1/3 cup shoyu or light
 soy sauce
2 teaspoons grated
 green ginger, to serve

400 g white boneless
 fish fillets, skinned,
 cut into 2 cm pieces

8 raw king (large)
 prawns, peeled,
 deveined with tails
 intact
8 scallops, cleaned
1 zucchini, cut into
 1 cm strips
1 red capsicum, cut into
 1 cm strips
4 button mushrooms,
 halved if large
8 green beans, in
 5 cm pieces
 flour for coating
vegetable oil for deep
 frying

1～To make Batter:
Place egg yolks in
mixing bowl, add iced
water; mix until well
combined. Add flour all
at once. Mix very lightly
with chopsticks or a
fork; the mixture will
still be lumpy.

**2～ To make Dipping
Sauce:** Combine all
ingredients except
ginger in small pan;
bring to boil. Remove
and keep warm. Place in
individual bowls. Serve
grated ginger separately.

3～Just prior to cooking
place fish fillet pieces in
iced water for about
5 minutes; drain and pat

dry on paper towels.

4～Lightly score
surface of prawns to
prevent curling when
cooking; pat dry with
paper towels. Dry
scallops; dust prawns
and scallops with flour.

5～Dust vegetables
lightly with flour. Fill a
large deep pan 2/3 full
with oil and heat to

moderately hot. Dip a
few vegetable pieces at a
time into batter and cook
2–3 minutes or until
lightly browned. Drain
on paper towels; keep hot.

6～Dip seafood into
batter. Cook a few
pieces at a time until
lightly browned. Drain
on paper towels. Serve
twith Dipping Sauce.

*Using a fork or chopsticks, mix the flour
into the egg mixture.*

*Combine all ingredients except ginger in a
pan and bring to boil.*

Seafood Tempura

Lightly score the surface of prawns with a knife to prevent them curling.

Dip floured vegetables into batter before cooking.

~ Fish and Chips ~

Preparation time:
15 minutes +
30 minutes standing
Total cooking time:
25 minutes

Serves 4

Beer Batter
1¼ cups plain flour
1 cup beer
2 eggs, separated
pinch salt
3 teaspoons oil

4 medium potatoes
oil for deep frying
4 white fish fillets,
skinned
cornflour for coating
lemon wedges, to serve

1. ~ **To make Batter:**
Place flour in small
mixing bowl. Make a
well in the centre; add
beer, egg yolks, salt and
oil. Gradually whisk flour
into egg mixture; beat to
form a smooth batter.
Cover; leave to stand for
30 minutes. Just before
using, beat egg whites in
a small bowl until firm
peaks form. Using a
metal spoon, fold egg
whites into batter.
2. ~ Peel potatoes; cut
into chips 1 cm thick.
Place in water until use.
3. ~ Fill a large, deep
pan ⅔ full with oil. Heat
to moderately hot. Drain
chips; dry on paper
towels. Cook chips in
batches 3–4 minutes or
until pale golden. Drain
on paper towels.
4. ~ Just before serving,
reheat oil. Re-cook chips
in batches until crisp and
golden. Drain; keep hot.
5. ~ Dry fish on paper
towels. Lightly dust with
cornflour; dip into batter.
Cook in hot oil 4–5
minutes until golden.
Drain on paper towels.
Serve with lemon wedges
and Remoulade sauce
(see page 2), if desired.

~ Smoked Trout Pâté ~

Preparation time:
10 minutes
Total cooking time:
nil

Makes 2 cups

250 g smoked trout,
skinned, boned
125 g butter, softened
125 g cream cheese,
softened
1 tablespoon lemon
juice
1 teaspoon horseradish
cream

¼ cup finely chopped
fresh parsley
¼ cup finely chopped
fresh chives
salt and freshly ground
black pepper, to taste
toasted brown bread, to
serve

1. ~ Place trout, butter
and cream cheese in
food processor. Process
for 20 seconds or until
mixture is smooth.
2. ~ Add lemon juice,
horseradish, parsley and
chives; process for
10 seconds. Add
seasoning and more
lemon juice, if desired.
3. ~ Transfer to small
serving dish. Serve with
hot toasted brown bread.
Note ~ Best on day of
preparation, but will keep
up to 4 days refrigerated.

Fish and Chips (top) and Smoked Trout Pâté

～ Scallops en Brochette ～

Preparation time:
25 minutes
Total cooking time:
5 minutes

Serves 6

¾ cup white wine	metal or soaked
1 tablespoon lemon	wooden skewers
juice	
36 scallops , cleaned	*Sauce*
1 cup parsley sprigs	1 small onion, finely
2 cloves garlic,	chopped
chopped	2 tablespoons white
4 slices bacon, cut into	wine vinegar
5 cm strips	⅓ cup thickened cream
30 g butter, melted	½ teaspoon cornflour
salt and black pepper	

1 ～ In a small pan, heat wine and lemon juice. Add scallops and simmer 1–2 minutes until just turning opaque. Drain and reserve poaching liquid.

2 ～ Combine parsley and garlic in food processor. Process 30 seconds or until finely chopped. Spread onto a flat plate. Roll scallops in parsley mixture until completely covered.

3 ～ Thread 6 scallops, alternating with pieces of rolled bacon, on skewers. Brush brochettes with melted butter; season with salt and pepper.

4 ～ **To make Sauce:** In a small pan, heat finely chopped onion, vinegar and ⅓ cup of the reserved poaching liquid. Boil mixture for 5 minutes or until reduced to 2 tablespoons. Blend cream and cornflour and add to mixture. Stir over low heat until mixture boils and thickens. Set aside and keep warm.

5 ～ Place brochettes under a preheated grill. Cook 4–5 minutes, turning frequently, until bacon is cooked. Serve immediately with freshly cooked pasta or on a bed of rice. Accompany with warm sauce in a serving jug.

Note ～ Brochettes and sauce may be prepared several hours ahead and refrigerated. Reheat sauce gently when required. Cook brochettes just prior to serving.

Variation ～ Instead of scallops you may use any firm white-fleshed fish which has been cut into cubes.

Drain cooked scallops and reserve poaching liquid for later use in sauce.

Roll scallops in combined finely chopped parsley and garlic.

Scallops en Brochette

Thread scallops alternately with rolled bacon onto skewers.

Add blended cream and cornflour to the reduced poaching liquid.

～ Gravlax ～

Preparation time:
**20 minutes +
marinating time**
Total cooking time:
nil

Serves 4–6

2 Atlantic salmon
  fillets, 300-400 g each
¼ cup caster sugar
¼ cup coarse sea salt
1 teaspoon white
  peppercorns, cracked
1 bunch fresh dill
cucumber and red
  capsicum slices,
  to serve
rye bread and crackers

Mustard Sauce
½ cup French mustard
1 teaspoon dry mustard
¼ cup honey
2 tablespoons tarragon
  vinegar
2 tablespoons fresh dill,
  chopped
⅓ cup oil

1 ～ Wash the fillets and pat dry on paper towels.
2 ～ In a small bowl combine sugar, salt and white peppercorns. Press the mixture onto flesh side of each fillet.
3 ～ Place one fillet flesh side up in shallow glass or ceramic dish. Cover thickly with dill sprigs. Place other fillet on top of the first fillet with the skin side up.
4 ～ Cover fish with plastic wrap and place a 1 kg weight on top of covered fish. Refrigerate 48 to 72 hours. Turn the fillets every 12 hours and at this point spoon some of the marinade, formed as fish stands, into the centre between the two fillets.
5 ～ **To serve**: Scrape off salt and dill mixture. Cut gravlax into very thin slices at an angle as you would cut smoked salmon. Serve with cucumber, capsicum and mustard sauce and accompany with rye bread and crackers.
6 ～ **To make Mustard Sauce**: Combine all the sauce ingredients except oil in food processor.

With motor running, gradually pour oil in thin stream through feed tube. Process until well combined and thick. Makes 1 cup.
Note ～ Sauce may be stored for one week, covered, in refrigerator. It can be frozen for up to one month.
To weight salmon for marinating, use a small breadboard with cans weighing 1 kg; place board with cans on top of salmon covered with plastic wrap.

Cover the salmon fillets thickly with sprigs of fresh dill.

After scraping off the salt and dill, cut the salmon into very thin slices.

Gravlax

～ Taramasalata ～

Preparation time:
25 minutes
Total cooking time:
Nil

Makes 1¹/₂ cups

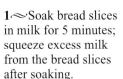

4 slices white bread, crusts removed	1 tablespoon grated onion
¹/₄ cup milk	¹/₂ cup olive oil
100 g tarama	¹/₃ cup lemon juice
1 egg yolk	black olives, to garnish
1 clove garlic, crushed	

1～Soak bread slices in milk for 5 minutes; squeeze excess milk from the bread slices after soaking.

2～Place the tarama and egg yolk in food processor. Process for 10 seconds.

3～Add drained bread, garlic and onion to tamara and egg yolk. Process for 20 seconds or until mixture is well combined and smooth.

4～With motor running, gradually add olive oil in a thin stream through feed tube. Process until all oil is absorbed.

5～Add lemon juice in small amounts, to taste.

Place mixture in a serving bowl. Garnish with black olives and serve with cucumber and slices of crusty bread.

Note～This is a classic Greek dish usually served as an appetiser or dip. Tarama is fish roe and is available from Greek specialty shops, most delicatessens and your local fishmonger. Taramasalata will keep refrigerated for up to one week stored in an airtight container. Bring to room temperature before serving.

You can serve this delicious appetiser in a number of ways, any of which will look very attractive on a serving platter. Taramasalata may be piped onto crispy bread, pitta or rye bread and garnished with parsley and capers. Alternatively, pipe the taramasalata into small pastry bases or fresh mushroom caps and garnish with fresh herbs.

Squeeze excess milk from the bread after soaking it.

Process tarama and egg yolk in food processor for 10 seconds.

Taramasalata

Add drained bread, garlic and onion to tamara mixture.

Add olive oil in a thin stream through feed tube with motor running.

~ Paella ~

Preparation time:
30 minutes + 2 hours soaking time
Total cooking time:
45 minutes

Serves 4

12 mussels, scrubbed, beards removed
$^{1}/_{2}$ cup white wine
1 small red onion, chopped
$^{1}/_{2}$ cup olive oil
1 small chicken breast fillet, cut into cubes
275 g raw medium prawns, shelled, deveined
100 g cleaned calamari, cut into rings
100 g white boneless fish, cut into cubes
$^{1}/_{2}$ small red onion, extra, finely chopped
1 slice bacon, finely chopped
4 cloves garlic, crushed

1 small red capsicum, finely chopped
1 tomato, peeled and chopped
$^{1}/_{2}$ cup fresh or frozen peas
90 g chorizo or peperoni, thinly sliced
salt and freshly ground black pepper, to taste
pinch cayenne pepper
1 cup uncooked long-grain rice
$^{1}/_{4}$ teaspoon powdered saffron
2 cups chicken stock, heated
2 tablespoons finely chopped fresh parsley

1 Soak the cleaned mussels for 2 hours in cold water. Discard any open or damaged mussels. Heat the wine and onion in a large pan. Add mussels, cover and shake the pan for 3–5 minutes over high heat. After 3 minutes start removing opened mussels and set aside; at the end of 5 minutes discard any unopened mussels. Reserve cooking liquid.
2 In a large frying pan heat half the oil. Pat chicken pieces dry with paper towels. Cook the chicken for 5 minutes or until golden brown. Remove from pan and set aside. Add prawns, calamari rings and fish pieces; cook 1 minute. Remove from pan and set aside.
3 Heat remaining oil in pan; add extra onion, bacon, garlic and capsicum to pan. Cook for 5 minutes or until onion is soft. Add tomato, peas, chorizo or peperoni, salt, black pepper and cayenne pepper. Add reserved cooking liquid; stir to combine. Add the rice and mix well.
4 Blend powdered saffron with $^{1}/_{2}$ cup of stock; add mixture with remaining stock to rice mixture; mix well. Bring slowly to the boil. Reduce heat to low and simmer rice mixture, uncovered, 15 minutes without stirring.
5 Place chicken pieces, prawns, calamari and fish on top of rice. Using a wooden spoon, gently push pieces into rice; cover and continue to cook over low heat for 10–15 minutes, or until rice is tender and seafood cooked. If rice is not quite cooked, add a little extra stock and cook for a few minutes more. Serve Paella in bowls, topped with mussels and sprinkled with parsley.
Note It's a good idea to purchase a few extra mussels to allow for any that do not open. Both black and green lip mussels are suitable for use in this recipe.

Paella

Add combined stock and powdered saffron to rice mixture.

Gently push chicken pieces, prawns, calamari and fish pieces into the rice.

~ Oysters ~

Most people buy fresh, opened oysters, but if keeping them for longer than a day, buy them unopened. Store, unrefrigerated, covered with a wet hessian or canvas bag, for up to 2 weeks.

Oysters au Naturel

Place 24 chilled fresh oysters in half shells on a bed of rock salt. Serve with Cocktail Sauce (see page 3), brown bread and butter, lemon wedges and ground black pepper. Serves 4.

Oysters Mornay

Melt 30 g butter in small pan. Stir in 1 tablespoon plain flour and cook for 2 minutes. Gradually add $2/3$ cup hot milk and stir over medium heat until mixture boils and thickens. Add salt, pepper and a pinch of cayenne pepper, to taste. Simmer the sauce very gently for 2 minutes, stirring occasionally. Stir in 1 tablespoon cream. Remove from heat and place plastic wrap on the surface to prevent a skin forming. Drain juice from 24 oysters in shells and add juice to sauce. Arrange oysters in shells on a bed of rock salt on an oven or grill tray.

Top oysters with a teaspoon of the hot sauce and sprinkle with $1/3$ cup grated cheddar cheese. Place under a preheated grill for 2–3 minutes or until lightly browned. Sprinkle with paprika. Serves 4.

Oysters Rockefeller

Arrange 24 fresh oysters in half shells on a bed of

rock salt. Cover and refrigerate. Melt 60 g butter in a pan. Add 2 slices finely chopped bacon and cook over medium heat until browned. Add 8 finely chopped English spinach leaves, 2 tablespoons finely chopped fresh parsley, 2 tablespoons finely chopped spring onions, 1/3 cup dry breadcrumbs and a drop of tabasco. Cook over medium heat for 5 minutes or until spinach is wilted. Top chilled oysters with spoonfuls of mixture; place under a preheated grill for 2–3 minutes or until lightly browned. Serves 4.

Oysters Kilpatrick
Place 24 fresh oysters on a grill tray. Heat 30 g of butter in a small pan. Add 2 tablespoons worcestershire sauce and simmer for 2 minutes. Spoon half a teaspoon of butter mixture onto each oyster. Sprinkle oysters with 3 slices of very finely chopped bacon and ground black pepper. Place under a preheated grill for 3–4 minutes or until bacon is crisp. Serve immediately on a bed of rock salt. Serves 4.

Angels on Horseback
Drain 24 bottled oysters on paper towels. Remove the rind from 6 slices of bacon. Divide slices into 4 pieces lengthways. Wrap a slice of bacon around each oyster and thread 2 wrapped oysters on each of 12 wooden skewers or toothpicks. Cook the skewered oysters under preheated grill, turning them occasionally, for 2–3 minutes or until bacon is cooked. Place skewers on buttered brown bread or toast. Grind black pepper over top; garnish with lemon wedges. Serve with sour cream. Serves 4.

From left to right:
Oysters au Naturel,
Oysters Rockefeller,
Angels on Horseback,
Oysters Mornay and
Oysters Kilpatrick

～ Spaghetti alla Marinara ～

Preparation time:
**40 minutes + 2 hours
soaking time**
Total cooking time:
50 minutes

Serves 4–6

12 mussels, scrubbed, beards removed	1/4 cup fish stock
	1 clove garlic, extra, crushed
Tomato Sauce	30 g butter
2 tablespoons olive oil	125 g calamari rings
1 onion, finely chopped	125 g boneless white
1 carrot, peeled and finely chopped	fish fillets, cut into cubes
1 red chilli, seeded and chopped	200 g raw medium prawns, shelled,
2 cloves garlic, crushed	deveined
425 g can tomatoes, crushed	1/2 cup fresh parsley, chopped
1/2 cup white wine	200 g can clams, drained
1 teaspoon sugar	375 g spaghetti
pinch cayenne pepper	
1/4 cup white wine, extra	

1 ～ Soak cleaned mussels for 2 hours in cold water. Discard open or damaged mussels.

2 ～ **To make Tomato Sauce:** Heat oil in a medium pan. Add onion and carrot; stir over medium heat 10 minutes or until lightly browned. Add chilli, garlic, tomato, white wine, sugar and cayenne pepper. Simmer, uncovered, 30 minutes, stirring occasionally.

3 ～ Meanwhile heat extra wine, stock and garlic in large pan. Add mussels, cover; shake over high heat for 3–5 minutes. After 3 minutes start removing opened mussels; set aside. After 5 minutes discard any unopened mussels. Reserve wine mixture.

4 ～ Melt butter in a frying pan. Add calamari rings, fish and prawns. Stir-fry for 2 minutes; set aside and keep warm.

5 ～ Add wine mixture, parsley, cooked seafood and clams to tomato sauce. Reheat gently.

6 ～ Cook pasta in a large pan of boiling water until tender. Drain. Combine sauce and pasta and serve.

Note ～ Tomato sauce may be made ahead. Complete dish just prior to serving.

Carefully remove the beards from the scrubbed shells.

Add white wine to pan containing other sauce ingredients.

Spaghetti alla Marinara

Cook for 3 minutes and then begin to remove any opened mussels.

Add prawns, fish and calamari rings to melted butter in pan.

～ Stuffed Calamari ～

Preparation time:
25 minutes
Total cooking time:
1 ½ hours

Serves 4–6

4–6 medium sized
  calamari tubes,
  cleaned

Stuffing
¼ cup olive oil
1 onion, finely chopped
2 cloves garlic, crushed
tentacles from squid,
  chopped (optional)
½ cup long-grain rice
2 tomatoes, peeled and
  chopped

⅓ cup pine nuts
⅓ cup currants
¼ cup finely chopped
  fresh parsley
salt and freshly ground
  black pepper

¼ cup olive oil, extra
½ cup white wine
1½ cups tomato juice,
  heated

---

1 ～ **To clean calamari:**
Pull away the insides,
including the quill, from
the body. Wash the
tubes thoroughly and,
using salt on hands to
make the task easier,
pull away the outside
skin. Rinse again and
dry on paper towels.
(Cleaned calamari may
also be purchased.
Simply wash the tubes
and pat dry.)
2 ～ **To make Stuffing**:
Heat the oil in a large
frying pan; add onion
and garlic and cook until
soft but not browned.
Add tentacles if using
(see Note), rice,
tomatoes, pine nuts,
currants, parsley, and
salt and pepper. Stir
to combine.
3 ～ Preheat oven to
moderate 180°C. Fill
calamari three-quarters
full with stuffing,
leaving room for the rice
to swell. Enclose the
open end using a needle
and cotton thread, or
a toothpick.

4 ～ Heat extra oil in
frying pan. Cook
calamari over high
heat for 2–3 minutes.
Transfer to an ovenproof
dish; add wine and hot
tomato juice. Cover and
cook for 1¼ hours or
until calamari is tender.
Remove, cut away thread
or take out toothpick.
Set aside; keep warm.
Reserve cooking liquid.
5 ～ Place reserved
liquid in a small pan;
bring to boil and boil for
10 minutes or until
sauce thickens and
reduces by half. Serve
calamari, thickly sliced,
with reduced tomato
sauce. Accompany with
snake beans and salad,
if desired.
Note ～ Stuffed
Calamari may be cooked
up to a day ahead and
then refrigerated. Reheat

with sauce in slow oven.
Do not freeze.
If calamari is purchased
with head attached, the
tentacles may be used.
Cut the head from the
tentacles just below the
eyes. Discard head,
remove beak from centre
of tentacles, trim off
suckers, chop tentacles
in small pieces.
Stuffing fills four 125 g
calamari hoods. If baby
calamari is used, mixture
fills 10–12 tubes.

Stuffed Calamari

Pull away the inside of the body from the calamari making sure to include the quill.

Stuff the calamari three-quarters full with stuffing, leaving room for rice to swell.

~ Ceviche (Marinated Fish Salad) ~

Preparation time:
**20 minutes +
marinating time**
Total cooking time:
Nil

Serves: 6

500 g firm white-fleshed
  fish, skinned, boned,
  cut into 1 cm cubes
200 g small scallops,
  cleaned
3/4 cup lemon juice
1 small red onion, finely
  chopped
1 red chilli, seeded and
  finely chopped
1–2 cloves garlic,
  crushed
2 tomatoes, seeded and
  chopped
1 tablespoon chopped
  fresh coriander
1 small cucumber,
  seeded, chopped into
  1 cm cubes
1/4 cup coconut cream
salt and freshly ground
  black pepper
3 avocados
fresh chives, to serve

1 ~ Combine fish cubes, scallops, lemon juice, finely chopped onion, chilli and crushed garlic in a ceramic or glass bowl. Cover with plastic wrap and chill for at least 6 hours or overnight, if possible. Stir mixture occasionally with a metal spoon, taking care not to break up the delicate fish flesh.

2 ~ Just before serving, drain the juice from seafood mixture and discard. Add chopped tomato, coriander, cubed cucumber, coconut cream, salt and freshly ground black pepper to the seafood mixture. Stir gently until just combined.

3 ~ Halve the avocados and remove stone. Roughly chop the flesh; add to salad mixture. Serve garnished with whole chives on a bed of radicchio lettuce, if desired.

Note ~ Ceviche, sometimes known as Cebiche or Seviche, originated in Latin America and is a classic method of preparing fish. The basis of the dish is raw fish marinated in lemon juice, or sometimes lime juice (or a mixture of the two), for several hours. During this time the acid in the juice acts to 'cook' the fish flesh, which gradually becomes opaque. Ceviche is usually served as a light, fresh first course, but it is also good on the buffet table or as part of a mixed seafood platter.

Clean the scallops before placing them in the marinade.

Add seeded and finely chopped chilli to the other ingredients.

Ceviche

Drain the juice from the seafood mixture just before serving.

Add the chopped avocado flesh to the seafood salad mixture.

～ Bouillabaisse ～

Preparation time:
40 minutes + 2 hours soaking
Total cooking time:
1 hour 10 minutes

Serves: 4–6

1.～Soak mussels for 2 hours in cold water. Discard open mussels.
2.～Place fish heads, bones, prawn and lobster shells in large pan. Add wine, water, onion, garlic and bay leaf. Bring to boil, reduce heat, simmer for 20 minutes. Strain and reserve liquid.
3.～Heat oil in large pan. Add extra onions, leek, and garlic. Cover and cook over low heat 20 minutes, stirring occasionally, until softened but not browned. Add tomato, tomato paste, saffron, bay leaves, basil, fennel seeds, rind, salt and pepper. Stir well, remove lid; continue to cook for 10 minutes, stirring frequently.
4.～Add reserved fish stock; bring to boil. Boil for 10 minutes, stirring often. Reduce heat; add fish pieces, lobster meat cut in 3 cm pieces and

12 mussels, scrubbed, beards removed
1–2 fish heads, with bones
500 g raw king (large) prawns, peeled, shells and heads retained
1 lobster tail, meat removed, shell retained
1 cup white wine
2 cups water
1/2 red onion, chopped
2 cloves garlic, chopped
1 bay leaf
1/4 cup olive oil
2 red onions, finely chopped, extra
1 small leek, finely sliced
4 cloves garlic, extra, crushed
4–6 tomatoes, skinned and chopped
3 tablespoons tomato paste

1/4 teaspoon saffron powder
2 bay leaves, extra
1 teaspoon dried basil leaves
1 teaspoon fennel seeds
5 cm piece orange rind
salt and freshly ground black pepper
500 g white fleshed fish, skinned, boned, cut into 3 cm pieces
1/2 cup fresh parsley, finely chopped

Rouille
4 thick slices white bread, crusts removed
water for soaking
4 cloves garlic, crushed
2 red chillies, finely chopped
2 egg yolks
salt and freshly ground black pepper
3/4 cup olive oil

mussels. Cover and simmer 4–5 minutes until mussels have opened (discard any unopened mussels). Add prawns and simmer, covered for 3–4 minutes or until just cooked.
5.～Remove rind and bay leaves. Transfer to serving bowls. Sprinkle with parsley. Serve with a spoonful of Rouille.

7.～**To make Rouille**: Place bread and water in bowl for 5 minutes. Squeeze water from bread. Place bread, garlic, chillies, yolks, salt and pepper in food processor. Process for 20 seconds. With motor running, add oil in slow stream. Process until thick. Place in serving bowl; cover and refrigerate until needed.

Bouillabaisse

Strain liquid from other ingredients and reserve it for later use.

Place bread, garlic, chillies, yolks, salt and pepper in food processor.

∽ Kedgeree ∽

Preparation time:
20 minutes
Total cooking time:
12 minutes

Serves: 4

500 g smoked haddock
  or cod
1 piece lemon rind
1 bay leaf
60 g butter
1 large onion, finely
  chopped
1 teaspoon curry
  powder
3 cups cooked Basmati
  rice, kept hot

3 hard boiled eggs,
  chopped
1/4 cup finely chopped
  fresh parsley
2 egg yolks
1/4 cup cream
1 lemon, quartered, to
  serve

1. ∽Place haddock or trevally in large pan with lemon rind and bay leaf. Cover with water. Bring to boil; simmer 6–8 minutes until cooked. Drain, skin, bone and flake fish; set aside. **2.** ∽Heat butter in large frying pan. Add onion and curry powder. Stir 5 minutes or until onion is soft, but not browned. **3.** ∽Add rice, eggs, parsley and combined egg yolks and cream. Mix until just combined. **4.** ∽ Serve very hot with lemon quarters and zucchini in flower, if desired.

∽ Marinated Octopus with Sweet Chilli Dressing ∽

Preparation time:
30 minutes
+ marinating time
Total cooking time:
4 minutes

Serves: 4–6

1 kg baby octopus
1/2 cup olive oil
2 cloves garlic, crushed
2 tablespoons finely
  chopped fresh
  coriander
1 red chilli, finely
  chopped
2 tablespoons lemon
  juice
metal skewers

Sweet Chilli Dressing
1 red chilli, finely
  chopped
1/4 cup lemon juice
2 tablespoons soft
  brown sugar
1 tablespoon fish sauce
2 tablespoons finely
  chopped fresh
  coriander
1 tablespoon sweet
  chilli sauce

1. ∽To clean octopus: Use a small sharp knife to cut off head; remove gut. Discard head and gut. Pick up octopus body and with your index finger push up the beak. Remove and discard beak. Clean octopus under running water and drain on paper towels. **2.** ∽In a glass or ceramic bowl combine oil, garlic, coriander, chilli and lemon juice.

Kedgeree (top) and Marinated Octopus with Sweet Chilli Dressing

Add octopus, mix well; cover and refrigerate overnight or for a minimum of 4 hours.
3 Drain octopus on paper towels. Thread 2 or 3 octopus pieces onto metal skewers.

Heat barbecue or grill plate to very hot. Coat plate with oil to prevent sticking. Cook, turning frequently, for 3–4 minutes. Coat with marinade often to keep octopus moist. Do not

overcook or octopus will toughen. Serve warm with dressing or cold as part of a salad.
4 **To make Dressing:** Combine all ingredients in a small screw-top jar; shake well.

～ Omelette Arnold Bennett ～

Preparation time:
10 minutes
Total cooking time:
10 minutes

Serves: 2

100 g smoked haddock	**1/2 cup grated gruyère**
30 g butter	**cheese**
2 tablespoons cream	**30 g butter, extra**
4 eggs, separated	**salt and freshly ground**
1/4 cup cream, extra	**black pepper, to taste**

1. ～Place haddock in small frying pan and cover with water. Bring slowly to boil; turn off heat. Cover pan and leave 10 minutes; drain. Skin fish, remove any bones and flake. Set aside.

2. ～Wipe out pan, return to heat; melt butter, add cream and flaked haddock. Stir over medium heat for 2–3 minutes. Leave mixture to cool.

3. ～In a small bowl beat egg yolks; add 1 tablespoon of the extra cream. In another bowl beat egg whites until soft peaks form. Fold in the yolks, haddock mixture and half the grated cheese.

4. ～Melt extra butter in medium non-stick frying pan. When hot, add egg mixture. Cook until golden and set on the bottom; do not fold.

5. ～Sprinkle with remaining cheese, pour remaining cream over. Add salt and pepper. Brown quickly under a preheated grill. Slide onto serving plate. Serve with lime wedges and mixed salad.

Note ～Haddock may be prepared ahead of time. Smoked haddock is popular throughout the world and adds a unique flavour to this classic dish. Arnold Bennett was a well known English novelist who died in 1931.

Remove any bones from the cooked fish and use a fork to flake.

Stir the fish, butter and cream mixture over medium heat.

Omelette Arnold Bennett

Fold in the yolks, haddock mixture and half the grated cheese.

Cook until the bottom of the omelette is set and golden.

~ Smoked Salmon ~

Not so long ago, smoked salmon was a rare luxury. It is now readily available in most supermarkets. This classic delicacy is best appreciated when served simply.

Smoked Salmon

Allow 30–60 g smoked salmon for each person. Serve thinly sliced and chilled with brown bread and butter, rye bread, Danish pumpernickel, water biscuits, blinis or toasted bread croûtes. Dress with a few drops of lemon juice, lemon wedges and freshly ground black pepper. Garnish with finely sliced onion or radish, pickled or fresh cucumber, capers, softened piped cream cheese or finely chopped fresh herbs.

Other uses for Smoked Salmon

Serve smoked salmon in sandwiches, pancakes, or quiches; on bagels, with cream cheese, capers, onion rings and fresh dill; with potatoes, salads, pasta, omelettes, and with scrambled or hardboiled eggs. It is excellent in paupiettes, mousses, dips and pâtés.

Sauces to accompany Smoked Salmon

Dill Sauce: Combine ⅓ cup mayonnaise, 2 teaspoons chopped fresh dill, 2 teaspoons lemon juice and a dash of tabasco. Sprinkle with fresh dill.

Horseradish & Chive Sauce: Combine ⅓ cup sour cream, 1 tablespoon horseradish,

2 teaspoons lemon juice, 2 tablespoons chopped fresh chives. Garnish with chives.

Gherkin & Dill Sauce:
Combine 1/3 cup sour cream, 2 teaspoons smooth mustard, 2 teaspoons chopped fresh dill, 2–3 teaspoons lemon juice and 2 small chopped gherkins.

Smoked Salmon with Blinis

Place 1 cup wholemeal or white self-raising flour, 1 teaspoon sugar and a pinch of salt in a bowl. Make a well in the centre. Combine 2 lightly beaten eggs, 1 tablespoon melted butter and 2 cups warm milk. Whisk liquid gradually into flour and mix to a smooth batter. Heat a heavy-based or non-stick frying pan and grease lightly with a little butter. Drop 2 teaspoons of batter in pan, making 4 or 5 blinis at a time. Cook until bubbles appear on the surface. Turn to brown other side. Transfer to plate. Cover and keep warm while cooking other blinis. Combine 100 g finely chopped smoked salmon with 250 g cottage cheese, 1/2 teaspoon lemon juice, 2 teaspoons grated onion and 1 teaspoon chopped

From bottom left, L to R: Dill Sauce, Gherkin & Dill Sauce, Horseradish & Chive Sauce; smoked salmon served on bagel, pumperknickel, blinis and crusty bread.

chives. Serve on top of hot blinis and sprinkle with paprika. Makes 25.

Smoked Salmon and Caviar with Blinis

Top blinis with some thinly sliced smoked salmon. Garnish with small slices of fresh lime and top each blini with a small mound of black (or red) caviar. Sprinkle with freshly ground black pepper.

~ Garlic Prawns ~

Preparation time:
30 minutes
Total cooking time:
6 minutes

Serves 6

1½ cups cooking oil
90 g butter
12 cloves garlic, peeled
3 small red chillies, seeded and finely chopped

30 raw medium king (large) prawns, shelled, deveined, tails intact
crusty French bread, to serve

1~ Pour oil into a large frying pan. Add butter to pan.
2~Crush garlic cloves into the pan. Add chilli to pan and stir.
3~ Heat frying pan and contents until butter is very hot and bubbling. Add the prawns and cook for 3–4 minutes or until prawns are pink and cooked.
4~Serve immediately with slices of fresh French bread.
Note~This classic Spanish dish is typically prepared in individual fireproof dishes. To prepare Garlic Prawns in this way, place ¼ cup

oil into each of 6 small fireproof dishes. Cut the butter into 6 cubes and add one cube to each dish. Crush 2 cloves of garlic into each dish.

Divide the chopped chilli into six portions and add to the bowls. Heat dishes and their contents until the butter is very hot and bubbling. Add 5 prawns to each dish. Cook prawns for 3–4 minutes or until they are pink and cooked through. Serve at once with French bread.

The barbecue is good for cooking Garlic Prawns as a direct flame is ideal for heating the oil and butter to a sufficiently high temperature. A cast iron pan is the best thing to use for cooking on the barbecue.

Peel and devein the prawns, leaving the tails intact.

Add chilli to the garlic, oil and butter mixture in the pan.

Garlic Prawns

Cook prawns for 3–4 minutes or until prawns are pink.

Slice French bread and serve with the very hot garlic prawns.

～ Seafood Chowder ～

Preparation time:
15 minutes
Total cooking time:
25–30 minutes

Makes: 10 cups

60 g butter	400 g firm white fish,
2 slices bacon, finely	skinned, boned and
chopped	cut into 2 cm cubes
1 leek, finely chopped	250 g scallops, cleaned
1 carrot, peeled and	200 g small prawns,
finely chopped	shelled, deveined
1 celery stalk, finely	1 cup cream
chopped	1/3 cup finely chopped
1 large potato, peeled	fresh parsley
and chopped	salt and freshly ground
1/3 cup plain flour	black pepper
4 cups hot fish	finely chopped parsley,
stock	extra, to garnish

1～Heat half the butter in a large pan, add bacon. Cook over low heat 5 minutes; remove bacon from pan and reserve. Add remaining butter, stir in the leek, carrot, celery and potato. Cook over medium heat, stirring frequently, for 5 minutes or until vegetables are softened and lightly golden.
2～Add flour, cook 1 minute; add heated fish stock gradually. Cook, stirring, 5 minutes or until mixture boils and thickens. Simmer over a low heat for 5 minutes, uncovered, stirring occasionally.

3～Add fish pieces and cook 5 minutes, stirring frequently. Add scallops, prawns, cream, parsley and reserved bacon. Mix well, cook 5 minutes without boiling. Add salt and pepper to taste. Serve immediately garnished with finely chopped fresh parsley.
Note～ Chowder may be made up to step 3 several hours ahead; cook fish and seafood just before serving. Chowders are hearty soups and make a delicious and filling meal when served with crusty bread.

Cook vegetables over medium heat until they are softened and lightly golden.

Add scallops, prawns, cream, parsley and cooked bacon to mixture in pan.

Seafood Chowder

~ Prawn Cocktail ~

Preparation time:
20 minutes
Total cooking time.
Nil

Serves 4–6

Cocktail Sauce
1 cup thick mayonnaise
2 tablespoons tomato
  sauce
2 tablespoons thick
  cream
dash tabasco sauce
1 teaspoon lemon juice
1 teaspoon
  worcestershire sauce

24 medium cooked
  prawns, shelled,
  deveined, tails intact
lettuce, for serving
lemon wedges, to serve
buttered brown bread,
  to serve

1 ~ To make Cocktail Sauce: Combine all sauce ingredients in large bowl. Mix well.
2 ~ Reserve 6–8 prawns; remove tails from the remaining prawns and add to the sauce. Mix gently.

3 ~ Arrange lettuce in serving dishes or bowls. Spoon prawn mixture into each dish. Decorate with reserved prawns. Serve with lemon

wedges and buttered brown bread.
Note ~ The cocktail sauce may be prepared several hours ahead and refrigerated.

~ Prawn Cutlets with Tartare Sauce ~

Preparation time:
**30 minutes +
refrigeration time**
Total cooking time:
10 minutes

Serves 4–6

24 raw medium king
  (large) prawns,
  shelled, tails intact
4 eggs
2 tablespoons soy sauce
cornflour for coating
dry breadcrumbs
oil for deep frying

Tartare Sauce
1 cup mayonnaise

1 tablespoon grated
  onion
1 tablespoon capers,
  chopped
1 tablespoon gherkins,
  finely chopped
1 tablespoon lemon
  juice
1 tablespoon finely
  chopped fresh parsley
dash tabasco sauce

1 ~ To butterfly prawns, slit open down back, remove vein and flatten gently with hand.
2 ~ Beat eggs and soy sauce in small bowl until combined. Dip prawns in cornflour, then in egg mixture and finally in dried breadcrumbs.

Refrigerate to firm up.
3 ~ Heat oil in deep pan until moderately hot. Deep fry prawns in batches until lightly golden. Drain on paper towels; serve with

tartare sauce and lemon wedges, if desired.
4 ~ To make Tartare Sauce: Combine all ingredients in medium bowl. Cover and refrigerate until needed.

Prawn Cocktail (top) and Prawn Cutlets with Tartare Sauce

~ Moules (Mussels) Marinière ~

Preparation time:
15 minutes
+ 2 hours soaking time
Total cooking time:
30–35 minutes

Serves: 4

24 prepared mussels (see Note)	**1 bay leaf**
1 onion, chopped	**50 g butter**
1 stick celery, chopped	**2 cloves garlic, crushed**
1 cup white wine	**2 onions, extra,** chopped
1½ cups fish stock	**1 teaspoon plain flour**
4 sprigs fresh parsley	**dill sprigs, to serve**
1 sprig fresh thyme	

1 Place prepared mussels, onion, celery and wine in a large pan; bring rapidly to boil. Cover and cook, shaking pan frequently, for 3 minutes. After 3 minutes start removing mussels as they open.

2 Pull away empty shells and discard. Set aside mussels attached to other shell half, cover and keep warm. After 5 minutes discard any unopened mussels.

3 Strain and reserve remaining liquid, discard vegetables.

4 In a pan heat fish stock, parsley, thyme and bay leaf. Bring to boil, reduce heat, cover and simmer 10 minutes. Remove herbs.

5 In a large pan heat butter. Add garlic and extra onion; cook gently 5–10 minutes or until onion is soft but not browned. Stir in flour. Add reserved mussel liquid and simmered fish stock. Bring to boil and simmer, uncovered, for 10 minutes.

6 Place mussels in four soup bowls. Ladle liquid over mussels and garnish with dill sprigs. Serve immediately with crusty bread.

Note To prepare mussels: Rinse the mussels several times under cold running water. Scrub each mussel with a stiff brush to remove any dirt. Pull out beard from between the shell halves. Cover mussels with water and soak for 2 hours. Discard any mussels that are not tightly closed. (It's a good idea to purchase a few extra mussels to allow for shells that don't open.) Rinse again before cooking. Always cook for a short time so that flesh doesn't toughen.

Prepare the mussels, onion and celery and place in a large pan with wine.

Pull away the empty side of the shell and discard; reserve shells containing mussels.

Moules (Mussels) Marinière

Strain remaining liquid from vegetables; reserve liquid and discard vegetables.

Cook onion and garlic until onion is soft; stir in flour.

~Lobster Thermidor~

Preparation time:
25 minutes
Total cooking time:
10–15 minutes

Serves: 2

1 medium cooked lobster	1 cup milk
60 g butter	3 tablespoons cream
4 spring onions, finely chopped	1 tablespoon chopped parsley
2 tablespoons plain flour	salt and freshly ground black pepper
1/2 teaspoon dry mustard	1/2 cup grated gruyère cheese
2 tablespoons white wine or sherry	1 tablespoon butter, extra

1. Using a sharp knife cut lobster in half lengthways. Remove tail meat, wash and set aside. Wash shells and set aside to drain. Slice lobster meat into 2 cm pieces, cover and refrigerate.
2. In a medium frying pan heat butter, add spring onions; cook for 2 minutes or until soft. Add flour and mustard, cook for 1 minute.

~Lobster Mornay~

Preparation time:
25 minutes
Total cooking time:
5–10 minutes

Serves 2

1 medium cooked lobster	2 tablespoons plain flour
1 1/4 cups milk	salt and white pepper
1 slice onion	pinch nutmeg
1 bay leaf	2 tablespoons cream
6 black peppercorns	1/2 cup grated cheddar cheese
30 g butter	

1. Using a sharp knife cut lobster in half lengthways. Lift the meat from the tail and body of the lobster. Crack the legs and prise the meat from them. Remove the intestinal vein and soft body matter and discard. Cut meat into 2 cm pieces, cover and refrigerate. Wash the shell halves, drain, dry and retain.
2. Heat milk, onion, bay leaf and peppercorns in small pan. Bring to boil. Remove from heat, cover; leave to infuse for 15 minutes. Strain.
3. Melt butter in large pan, add flour, stir for 1 minute. Remove from heat; gradually add milk. Whisk until smooth. Cook, whisking over medium heat, until mixture boils and thickens. Season with salt, pepper and nutmeg. Stir in cream.
4. Fold lobster meat through the sauce. Divide mixture into shells; sprinkle top with cheese. Place under a preheated grill for 2 minutes or until cheese is melted. Serve.

Lobster Thermidor (top) and Lobster Mornay

Gradually stir in wine and milk; cook, stirring, until mixture boils and thickens. Simmer 1 minute. Stir in cream, parsley, lobster meat and season to taste. Heat gently.

3 Spoon into lobster shells, sprinkle with cheese, dot with extra butter. Place under preheated grill 2 minutes or until lightly browned.

Note Sauce may be prepared several hours ahead and refrigerated. Reheat sauce gently.

～ Honey Prawns ～

Preparation time:
20 minutes
Total cooking time:
12 minutes

Serves 4

16 raw king (large) prawns, shelled, deveined, tails intact 1/4 cup cornflour ***Batter*** 1 cup self-raising flour 1/4 cup cornflour, extra	1 cup water 1/4 teaspoon lemon juice 1 tablespoon oil 1/4 cup honey oil for deep frying 1/4 cup sesame seeds, lightly toasted

1 ～ Pat prawns dry using paper towels then lightly dust them with the cornflour.

2 ～ **To make Batter**: Sift the flour and extra cornflour into a medium bowl. Combine water, lemon juice and oil. Make a well in the centre of the flour and gradually add the liquid, beating well to make a smooth batter.

3 ～ Place honey in a large pan and heat over very gentle heat. Remove from heat and keep warm.

4 ～ Heat the oil in a large, deep frying pan utnil moderately hot.

Dip prawns in the batter; drain excess. Using tongs or a slotted spoon, place prawns, a few at a time, in hot oil. Cook for 2–3 minutes or until prawns are crisp and golden. Drain on paper towels and keep warm.

5 ～ Place cooked prawns in the pan with the warmed honey; toss gently to coat. Remove, place on serving plate and sprinkle with sesame seeds. Serve immediately.

Note ～ Honey Prawns is a classic Chinese dish. Honey, one of the oldest sweeteners known to man, has been used in cooking since ancient times. When warming it, don't overheat or it will caramelise and lose some of its flavour.

Pat the king prawns dry with paper towels before dusting with cornflour.

Make a well in the centre of the flour and gradually add the liquid.

Honey Prawns

Place prawns in hot oil and cook until crisp and golden.

Toss the cooked prawns gently in the warmed honey.

~ Coquilles Saint Jacques ~

Preparation time:
20 minutes
Total cooking time:
10 minutes

Serves 4

1 cup fish stock
1 cup white wine
500 g scallops, cleaned
  and cut in half
60 g butter
4 spring onions, chopped
1 slice bacon, finely
  chopped
100 g button mushrooms,
  thinly sliced

¹/4 cup plain flour
³/4 cup cream
1 teaspoon lemon juice
salt and freshly ground
  black pepper
1 cup fresh
  breadcrumbs
30 g butter, melted,
  extra

1~Grease 4 small heatproof dishes or scallop shells. Heat fish stock and white wine in medium pan; add the prepared scallops. Cover, simmer over medium heat 4 minutes or until scallops are opaque. Remove scallops with slotted spoon; cover and set aside. Bring liquid in pan to boil and reduce until 1¹/2 cups remain.

2~Melt butter in medium pan. Add the spring onions, bacon and sliced mushrooms. Cook over medium heat 3 minutes, stirring occasionally, until soft but not brown.

3~Stir in flour, cook 2 minutes. Add reduced stock, stir until mixture boils and thickens. Stir in cream, lemon juice, salt and pepper. Cover; set aside. Keep warm.

4~In a small bowl combine breadcrumbs and extra butter.

5~Divide scallops between the 4 dishes. Spoon warm sauce over scallops, sprinkle with breadcrumb mixture. Place under preheated grill until breadcrumbs are browned. May be served with mandarin segments and coral lettuce, if desired.

Note~Recipe can be made several hours ahead up to Step 5 and refrigerated. Heat the sauce gently before completing dish. Do not overcook scallops, otherwise they will toughen. Dish can be finished in the oven rather than under grill, if preferred. Heat oven to moderate 180°C; cook for 5 minutes or until top is browned. Serve immediately.

Remove scallops with slotted spoon and reserve the cooking liquid.

Cook spring onions, bacon and mushrooms in butter over medium heat.

Coquilles Saint Jacques

～Stock and Court Bouillon～

Fish stock makes a nutritious base for delicious seafood soups and adds subtle flavour and richness to sauces. Court bouillon in its various forms is an ideal poaching medium for seafood.

Fish Stock (Fumet de Poisson)

Place 1 kg of fish heads, bones and trimmings (no skins), 1 sliced onion, 1 sliced carrot, 1 sliced stick celery, 2 bay leaves, 1 sprig each of parsley and thyme, 1/4 teaspoon salt and 2 litres of water in a large pan. Bring slowly to boil over low heat. Skim off scum as it rises to surface. Cover pan and simmer for about 15 minutes. Add 1 cup white wine and 6 black peppercorns. Replace lid and simmer for another 5 minutes. Strain mixture through a muslin-lined strainer; take care not to press solids down or you will make the stock cloudy. Discard solids and cool stock quickly by pouring small amounts into containers and placing them in the refrigerator. Makes 2 litres.

This stock will keep for 2 days in the refrigerator and may also be frozen for up to 2 months. Freeze in containers to suit your needs: ice cube containers for flavouring a fish sauce, 1 or 2-cup capacity containers for soups. You may also reduce stock to use as a base for sauces.

Court Bouillon

This may be used as an all-purpose poaching liquid to cook and flavour fish and shellfish. When poaching, make sure liquid does not boil or it

may cause seafood to toughen and break up.

Place 1 sliced onion, 1 sliced carrot, 1 sliced celery stick, 1 bay leaf, 1 sprig each of parsley, thyme and dill, 1/4 teaspoon salt and 6 cups of water in a large pan. Bring slowly to boil over low heat. Simmer, covered, for 15 minutes. Add 1 cup white wine, 6 white peppercorns, and 1 clove of garlic (optional) to pan and simmer for another 15 minutes. Cool slightly and strain. Store in the refrigerator for up to5 days. May be frozen in small containers for up to 2 months. Makes 2 litres.

Red Wine Court Bouillon

Instead of white wine in the recipe for Court Bouillon, use 1 cup of red wine. This version would be most suitable for strongly flavoured oily fish, such as mullet. Add the fish to the prepared court bouillon and poach until fish is cooked through.

Vinegar Court Bouillon

Replace wine in Court Bouillon recipe with 200 ml of red or white vinegar. Add the vinegar with the vegetables and water and simmer for 30 minutes. Add seafood of your choice and poach until just cooked.

For best results, use only the freshest ingredients for making your own seafood stocks. Easy and satisfying to prepare, they are worth the effort.

Milk and Lemon Court Bouillon

This version of court bouillon is used for poaching salted or smoked fish as the milk helps remove strong flavours. It is best made just prior to use and is not suitable for freezing.

Combine 1 1/4 cups milk, 5 cups water, and 1/4 teaspoon salt in a large pan. Add 1 peeled, sliced lemon and heat to a gentle simmer. Add preferred seafood and poach to taste.

∼ Index ∼

Front cover, clockwise from top left: Prawn cocktail (page 52), Oysters au Naturel, Oysters Rockefeller and Oysters Mornay (page 32), Paella (page 30), Lobster Thermidor (page 56)